T0147182

Oh, Taste and See

The Poetry Is Good

STEPHANIE RIDGEWAY-HOGAN

WESTBOW
PRESS®
A DIVISION OF THOMAS NELSON
& ZONDERVAN

WestBow Press books may be ordered through booksellers or by contacting:

WestBow Press
A Division of Thomas Nelson & Zondervan
1663 Liberty Drive
Bloomington, IN 47403
www.westbowpress.com
844-714-3454

ISBN: 978-1-6642-5022-2 (sc)
ISBN: 978-1-6642-5023-9 (hc)
ISBN: 978-1-6642-5021-5 (e)

Library of Congress Control Number: 2021923505

Print information available on the last page.

WestBow Press rev. date: 11/29/2021

Contents

Dedication vii

Appreciation ix

Preface xiii

Introduction xv

The Brother Was Fine! 1

Making Up 3

Love 5

The Most Loved of All Creatures 7

Living with Purpose 9

Love Is in the Air. 11

Lovemaking 13

Love Expressions 15

The Power of a Hug. 17

Heart's Strong Tower 19

Oh, Breath of Life. 21

The Beauty of It All 23

I Stand in Awe 25

Unconditional 27

Long-Suffering 29

Trust Issues 31

Nurtured by Love 33

Let's Wait 35

Flames of Desire. 37

The Love of My Life. 39

Crab Legs 41

Dot 43

Rain on Me 45

Pregnancy 47

Your Creation Is Amazing 49

Limits 51

How Long? 53

Beauty and Brains 55

What Did I Do? 57

Cold 59

Whom Can You Trust? 61

Molested 63

Reminder 65

Marvelous 67

In the Heat of the Moment 69

Beaten Down 71

Hustle 73

The Vindicator 75

Sweet 77

Epilogue 79

Works Cited 81

About the Author 83

Notes 85

Dedication

This book is dedicated to my heavenly Father, the Holy Spirit, and the Lord Jesus Christ. They have been my strength throughout my salvation walk. When friends were not there to encourage or uphold me, the Lord helped me to bear my cross. I have been taught to give honor where honor is due. I am nothing without my Savior.

Appreciation

I express sincere gratitude to WestBow Press for doing such an outstanding job on this book project. Your professionalism is commendable. I'd like to also thank all of the pastors I've had in my life over the years who taught me God's holy word. I am grateful for your dedication to the gospel.

But the fruit of the Spirit is love, joy, peace, patience, kindness, goodness, faithfulness, gentleness, self-control; against such things there is no law.

Galatians 5:22–23 ESV

Oh! Taste & See!

Preface

The goal of this book is to express appreciation for the things God has created, to make you laugh, and to bring deliverance to the hurting soul. Pain doesn't ever feel as bad when others have gone through, or are going through, similar circumstances as we are. In our pursuit of Christ, we must not forget our humanity. Christ became human to identify with humanity. The Creator became the created. I hope this book will make you laugh, consider your ways, exhale, and know that it is all right to go through trials as long as you don't allow trials to break you and rob you of your faith.

Introduction

All the poems in this book express a life event or thought I have experienced or that someone I know has experienced. The book expresses an appreciation for all that God has created. The title of the book came to me as I thought about the Lord's goodness. In Psalm 34:8, David said, "O Taste and see that the Lord is good" (Psalm 34:8 KJV). Of course, we know that David didn't literally taste the Lord. The nonliteral language expresses that if God could be tasted, he would taste phenomenal because of his mighty acts. Who doesn't like food? Food is enjoyed across all cultures. God's love, mercy, and kind acts are flavorful, and so is the book of poems, *Oh, Taste and See: The Poetry Is Good!* These poems express an appreciation for God Most High's creation. Read the book yourself and then recommend it to a friend. I am sure you will not regret it.

Many of the poems will make you laugh, cry, and ponder the meaning. Enjoy!

Suggestion: Before you begin reading, think about all the things you love and enjoy. Then think about all the things that have brought you pain.

MAKE LOVE -not- WAR

love you

be my Valentine

THINKING OF YOU

you & me

you are the best

I love you

you -and- me

Love

LOVE is in the air

I love you

Hugs and kisses

with love

you are the best

Happy Valentine's Day

love is in the air

xoxo

you Make -ME- feel so loved

YOU are loved

I ♥ you

FOR YOU with love

I love you

Share -THE- love

thank you for being in my life

love you

Stephanie Ridgeway-Hogan

The Brother Was Fine!

Forget the six-pack;
The brother was packing a twelve.
From head to toe, he was built!

For a moment, I forgot my salvation.
I gave him a gaze and knew I needed
Some reformation.

It wasn't a sin to look once since he was in view.
But I had to fight some serious demons
Not to take look number two.

Oh! Taste & See!

Stephanie Ridgeway-Hogan

Making Up

Lips touching, smooth and luscious.
Whispers in my ear, bringing me chills.

Warm hands on my skin.
Temperature now rising.
Eyes now glaring into mine.
Nothing despising.

Making up was well worth the fight.
Now let's get angry again
And apologize until morning light.

Oh! Taste & See!

Love

When I think of love, I think of you.
I think of beauty, gentleness, and jealousy.

When I think of love, I think of you.
I think of generosity, sacrifice, and triumph.

When I think of love, I think of you.
I think of passion, intimacy, and resilience.

When I think of love, I think of you.
I think of caring, sharing, and joy.

When I think of love, I think of you—
And only you—
For you are love.

Oh! Taste & See!

Stephanie Ridgeway-Hogan

The Most Loved of All Creatures

If I could choose to be any creature,
I would choose to be the most loved creature,
Not a dog, not an elephant, or a rat.

I would choose to be the best loved creature,
Not a giraffe, not a wolf, or a cat.

I would choose to be the highest loved creature,
Not a bird, not a lion, or a bat.

I would choose to be the utmost loved creature,
Not a tiger, lion, or bear.

I'd choose to be human all over again
From the beginning of the world until its end.

No creature is lovelier
Than the one the Creator laid down His life for.
In His image I was created.

Oh! Taste & See!

Stephanie Ridgeway-Hogan

Living with Purpose

I have seen in nature things both great and small,
But the honeybee has the most amazing fate of them all.

A tiny thing, I must say, with such a big job to do.
The queen mates with a colony to feed honey to me and you.

The drone male dies after mating.
He's done with his job of sperm donating.

The worker bees regulate the sex of unborn eggs
By sizing cells in a hive.
Then the queen stops by to fertilize.

Unfertilized eggs become drones,
While fertilized eggs become female strong.

Honey, beeswax, pollen, royal jelly—
Some of the things we use to stay healthy.

Honeybees intuitively know their purpose.

Oh! Taste & See!

Stephanie Ridgeway-Hogan

Love Is in the Air

I can feel it rushing over me,
A sweet, gentle breeze that sets my mind at ease.
Inhale the fragrance; saturate yourself in it.
Love is in the air; embrace it and submit!

Blow the fragrance of love like a rushing wind.
Spread the fresh scent!
Melt a heart wherever you go.
Its power transforms the cruel,
Heals the hurting,
Brings peace and tranquility,
Empowers the insecure!
Love is in the air
Only where you carry it!

Love starts with you!

Oh! Taste & See!

Stephanie Ridgeway-Hogan

Lovemaking

Kisses on your neck, warm, tender, and satisfying.
My hands on your chest, massaging you,
Working my way to the Southern Hemisphere.
Finally reaching the South Pole,
Chills on arrival.
Suddenly, body temperature rising.

Blanketed by your warm embrace,
Hand-and-glove fit.
Welcomed wrestling match
Then deep sleep.

Nestled in your arms when I awake,
Staring into your gorgeous face.
Ready for round two
With my soul mate.

Be fruitful, multiply, replenish the earth.

Oh! Taste & See!

Stephanie Ridgeway-Hogan

Love Expressions

A ring! A flower! Sweet perfume!
Holding hands! Kissing! Dinner for two!

You serving me,
And me serving you!

Love expressions!

Oh! Taste & See!

Stephanie Ridgeway-Hogan

The Power of a Hug

Was it a rough day at work?
Let's not talk about it now; just hug me.

Did the teacher call today?
Let's talk about it later; just hug me.

Did the doctor call with my evaluation?
Let's not talk about it now; just hug me.

Hug me tightly, hug me long, hug away my pain.
Sing me a love song.

Hug me in adversity; hug me in celebration.
Hug me! Hug me! Hug me!

Oh! Taste & See!

Stephanie Ridgeway-Hogan

Heart's Strong Tower

I tried to climb the high walls
To overtake the fenced city.
It was well guarded by old lovers.

Every time I tried to enter the high gates undercover,
To rescue her from her pain,
She mistook me for the men who abused her,
Used her,
Lied to her,
Cheated on her.
Therefore, she ran me off.

Had she looked closer,
Outside the fortress she had built,
She would have noticed that true love awaited.

But she kept mistaking me for Mr. Abuser,
Mr. User, Mr. Liar, Mr. Cheater, and Mr. Rape.

So here I stand, hoping one day she'll let me protect her heart
Within the gates.

Oh! Taste & See!

Stephanie Ridgeway-Hogan

Oh, Breath of Life

I bought her diamonds, rubies, and pearls.
I bought her houses, cars, and land.
I took her here and there and everywhere.

All I ever wanted was someone to hold my hand.
He should have given me support in adversity,
Helped me study for my tests.
He should have given me foot massages.
He should have brought lunch to my job
While I was confined to the premises.

All I ever wanted was love and the simple things in life—
Cuddling, watching TV, cooking dinner together,
Laughter from dawn to sunset, occasional travel,
Common interests and a few material pleasures.

Gifts without love and affection are
like a body without breath.
Breathe breath of life.

Oh! Taste & See!

Stephanie Ridgeway-Hogan

The Beauty of It All

Sitting on a boulder overlooking the ocean,
Before me displayed was the most beautiful horizon.

The sun appeared to sink into the water.
Colors so magnificent going in straight lines across the sky.

Shades of gray, orange, blue, purple, and gold.
What a lovely sight to behold.

As I sat there, taking it all in, I wondered within myself,
Who is this great Creator?
Why does he keep himself hidden?
Why doesn't he make himself visible, to
take credit for what he did?

As I sat in awe of it all, as I had many times before,
Amazed as if it were the first-time
watching creation fold and unfold.

Nature displays the Creator's glory.
He is hidden but clearly visible.

Oh! Taste & See!

Stephanie Ridgeway-Hogan

I Stand in Awe

The greatness of his mind, who can fathom?

Take a visit to the ocean floor, and you
will gasp because it's insane.
The Creator makes so much visible,
but invisible thus he remains.

The rain forest is filled with many
beautiful living things to include
Diverse plants, flower, animals, insects,
berries, fruits, nuts, trees—
A vast multitude of everything.

The stars, planets, and heavenly bodies
Are amazing to behold.
The Creator spins the earth extremely fast without anyone
falling off or getting dizzy.
Certainly he is not like man; he deserves recognition.

Oh! Taste & See!

 Stephanie Ridgeway-Hogan

Unconditional

You love me so much
Though I have broken all your rules.

Who has ever heard of such?
You cared for me when I didn't know your name.

What's in it for you?
This has got to be some kind of game.

You give so much, yet you ask for so little—
Love unconditionally.

Oh! Taste & See!

Stephanie Ridgeway-Hogan

Long-Suffering

Wandering eyes when he thinks no one is watching,
Slipping the waiter his number.
Lips dripping with lies,
Hopeful, wanting to believe, that he'll someday change.

Got a thought: Why don't I just dump
him and get someone else?
There must be something better on the shelf.

[Sighs] Relationships are not without drama.
God understands; He is married too.
He puts up with lies and cheating
And a lot more than we do.

Oh! Taste & See!

Trust Issues

I love you, baby.
I trust you too.

I need you, baby.
I can't live without you.

I would sail the seven seas to be with you, baby.
You have my heart and soul.

I trust you, baby.
Not!
Let's stop the nonsense.
I just love you.

Oh! Taste & See!

Nurtured by Love

I felt like a flower that had been picked
From a field of beautiful flowers.
Out of all the colors, shapes, sizes, and fragrances,
He picked me.

He held me.
He gently touched my petals.
He placed his nose close to me to absorb my fragrance,
A fragrance of sweetness from the scent of love,
A fragrance of bitterness from the stems and roots
Because of the pain I had endured.

A fragrance of hope
Because he placed me in a vase of fresh water,
Fertilized by his nurture and care.

Oh! Taste & See!

Stephanie Ridgeway-Hogan

Let's Wait

Like delicious chocolate
But sweet to my ears
Were the words he whispered.
Soft, gentle, and ever so clear.

Tantalizing warm breaths made me quiver
As he asked, "Can I taste and touch
You here and here?"

I responded,
"No! Not yet, my dear.

Let's wait until the honeymoon to experience bliss and
Two hearts filled with cheer.

Thus the Creator will be pleased with our self-control
For reverencing a name
We both extol.

The fire of our passion will be worth the wait
When we come together to consume each
other like a meal on a dinner plate."

Oh! Taste & See!

 Stephanie Ridgeway-Hogan

Flames of Desire

I felt him watching me from across the room.
I looked to gaze upon his face.
His eyes said more than his
Mouth would ever speak.
A glance of satisfaction.

Silent words I felt, *Can I undress you?*
Can I take you there?
Can we make love tonight?

For a moment I felt like a rack
Of baby back ribs
As his eyes burned with fire.

I accepted the fact that I must have been looking
Mighty good and refused to give in to his desire.

Oh! Taste & See!

Stephanie Ridgeway-Hogan

The Love of My Life

Beautiful, so full of love,
Admiration for him,
The One above.

He loves me with all my flaws.
I love him with my all and all.

My protector, my joy, my peace,
My King, my friend.
His love for me
Never ends.

Oh! Taste & See!

Crab Legs

Hard on the outside,
Soft inside.

Crack them open—
Sweet, tender meat.

Dipped in butter,
Melts in your mouth.
Tastebuds aroused.

Oh! Taste & See!

Stephanie Ridgeway-Hogan

Dot

Don't mess with me.
My stomach is cramping;
My head is hurting.
My emotions are running rampant.

I love you dearly.
You know I do.
But on days like these,
I'm entitled to be blue
Dot.

Oh! Taste & See!

Stephanie Ridgeway Hogan

Rain on Me

Let your love rain on me
Like a spring shower,
Renewing dead things,
Refreshing the hour.

Let your love rush over me
Like an ocean wave
Pushing to shore.

Living waters,
Let your love rush over me
Like a mighty wind
Blowing away all sin.

Let your love rain on me
Again and again.

Oh! Taste & See!

Stephanie Ridgeway-Hogan

Pregnancy

Your house is like a birthing room,
Souls pushed out unto salvation.
Umbilical cord cut from an old life,
Your word washing away all filth.
Reborn, reborn, reborn.

Oh! Taste & See!

Your Creation Is Amazing

The beauty of creation is amazing,
Like clouds in the sky are amazing.

The beauty of creation is amazing,
Like flowers blooming are amazing.

The beauty of creation is amazing,
Like Venus flytraps are amazing.

The beauty of creation is amazing,
Like precious stones are amazing.

The beauty of creation is amazing,
Like the galaxy is amazing.

The beauty of creation is amazing,
Like a web spun by a spider is amazing.

Amazing is creation
Because God is amazing.

Oh! Taste & See!

Stephanie Ridgeway-Hogan

Limits

You cheated on me,
Yet I still loved you.

You lied to me,
Yet I still loved you.

You didn't support me,
Yet I still loved you.

You watched me struggle,
Yet I still loved you.

You left me,
Yet I still loved you.

You wanted to come back.
I refuse to put myself through the same pain,
Yet I still loved you.

Love has no limits.
Limits must be placed on abusers of love.

Oh! Taste & See!

How Long?

I've been single for quite some time.
I am longing for someone to be mine.

I sleep holding my pillow tight.
I wake to the lonely morning light.

Another wretch undone I don't want to meet.
Nonetheless, desperation won't let him take a seat.

I've learned my lesson far too many times,
Trying to appease loneliness while paying the fine.

What is the price one must pay
In order for patience to have her way?

Another lonely night it will be
Until Mr. Worthy finally finds me.

How long?
However long it takes.

Oh! Taste & See!

Beauty and Brains

Whoever thought that it would be difficult
To be smart and beautiful?

Always loving and caring, but who can see your kindness,
For your brains and beauty?

Submit if you will.
Give all you can.
Most of the time, it will not be received with cheer
Due to your brains and beauty.

Despised, although a heart filled with love,
Hindered by your brains and beauty.

The things we take for granted others notice
While coveting your beauty and brains.

Give your life to serving others.
Brains and beauty will make it appear all in vain.
Oh, I didn't see your good works for your brains and beauty!

Everything beautiful is not shallow.
Everyone who is smart is not a know-it-all.
Look beyond the surface and you'll find
What's in the heart.

Oh! Taste & See!

Stephanie Ridgeway-Hogan

What Did I Do?

Kind, caring, thoughtful, generous
Easygoing.
People will still press your buttons.

Is it the thrill of having power that people are mean?
They find a way to start trouble.

Loving, cheerful, gentle, patient,
Disgruntled people don't respond to it positively.

"What did I do?" you ask yourself over and over.

You didn't do a thing!
The miserable hates the joyful,
Thus they push your buttons.

Oh! Taste & See!

Cold

Icy, chilly, cold, freezing.
Glacier, ice, snow, hail.

Icebox, deep freezer, cooler.
Popsicle, ice cream, ice chiller.

The heart that can no longer love
Cold.

Oh! Taste & See!

Whom Can You Trust?

Whom can you trust at the beginning of the day?

Is it your mama who lied?

Is it your daddy who tried?

Is it your granny who overworked you?

Is it your uncle who wants nothing to do with you?

Is it your aunt who never responds back?

Is it the lover who ran off with Jack?

Is it your friend who slept with your man?

Whom can you trust in the end?

Love everyone.

Trust no one.

What a friend we have in Jesus!

Oh! Taste & See!

Stephanie Ridgeway-Hogan

Molested

I was but a child,
Innocent, naive, trusting.
You were an adult.
You desired but a babe with your lusting.

Oh! Taste & See!

Stephanie Ridgeway-Hogan

Reminder

A variety of colors
Decorate the sky.
A covenant between the Creator and man;
Total water destruction will not happen again.
Communicating beauty and forgiveness,
A rainbow!

Oh! Taste & See!

Marvelous

I stand amazed at the gifts in humankind.
Every make and model you can imagine,
Big, medium, and small engines.
To think this is not all that will be designed;
There is still more to discover.
The Creator's riches are unsearchable.

Oh! Taste & See!

Stephanie Ridgeway-Hogan

In the Heat of the Moment

In the heat of the moment,
I produced you.
I did not have the slightest clue.

The passion got the better of me.
It felt like love.

I was left to raise you alone.
Now every time I look at you,
I am reminded of the heat of the moment.

The moment brought forth both pain and joy—
The joy of having a child,
The pain of raising you alone,
The joy of watching you play,
The pain of struggling to provide for you.

The heat of the moment made me believe a lie,
A lie that will come back to haunt me.

I can hear the question replaying in my mind:
"Mom, where is my dad?"

Oh! Taste & See!

Stephanie Ridgeway-Hogan

Beaten Down

Beaten down by lack,
Having to sleep with man after man to have my back.

No education, no experience, dead-end jobs,
Living life with deep sobs.

Pillow wet with tears daily.
Can you now hear my ukulele?

It plays the tune of the blues.
It tells of bitter stories I've accrued.

If only I had listened to the Author of life,
I wouldn't feel so beaten down.

Oh! Taste & See!

Stephanie Ridgeway-Hogan

Hustle

Nine to five, side hustle, small-business owner,
Also collecting coins as a blood donor.

Trying to keep my head above water,
Using money as a tool, not being a hoarder.

No ride or die; just me and my Creator
Pushing hard to avoid traitors.

I am making it in these streets without selling my soul
To the devil.

Oh! Taste & See!

Stephanie Ridgeway-Hogan

The Vindicator

He left me high and dry.
I busted my rear to help him fly.

He moved on quickly with another lover,
Forgot about me overnight as I would soon discover.

Now I live wanting revenge.
He must pay for what he did.

I followed the procedures of wifely duties.
In return, he ran around chasing _____.

Trouble doesn't last always.
This too shall pass.
In the end I will show him I am one
Bad class.

The table is prepared before my enemies.
I will be still, and render God's remedies.

I am coming out
On top.
God is my vindicator.

Oh! Taste & See!

Stephanie Ridgeway-Hogan

Sweet

Pear, apple, orange, plum,
Watermelon, mango, papaya,
Pineapple, dragonfruit, apricot,
blackberry, raspberry,
Strawberry, grapes, kiwi.
Like the juices from fruits running down my lips,
So sweet is your love!

Epilogue

Prayer of Blessings:

Heavenly Father, I come to you in the name of Jesus. Forgive me of all sins and the iniquities of my forefathers. I renounce every evil practice that I have committed against you in the form of pride, lust of the eyes, and lust of the flesh, for this is all there is in the world according to scripture. Fill me with the Holy Ghost, which is my seal that I'm your possession. Keep me from sinful desires that war against my soul. Teach me your Word so that my feet are founded upon the Rock in the days of adversity. Help me to form the kind of relationship with you that the spirit world recognizes and respects because of my affiliation with Christ. Give your angels charge over me. Destroy the principalities, powers, rulers of darkness, and spiritual wickedness in high places on my behalf that I may obtain all you desire for me. Grant your goodness and mercy to follow me and my household all the days of our lives. Place my name in your Book of Life. Keep me from evil. Cause my hands to do exploits and cause your gifts in me to make room for me. Help me to follow you all the days of my life. Manifest the fruit of the Spirit in my life and in the lives of my loved ones. In Jesus's name I pray, Amen!

Works Cited

Bible Hub: English Standard Version, 2004–2021. www. biblehub.com.

Bible Hub: King James Version, 2004–2021. www.biblehub.com.

About the Author

Stephanie Ridgeway was born and raised in Butler, Alabama. She currently lives in Columbia, South Carolina. She has traveled nationally and abroad. She has spent more than twenty years of her life working in public education. She continues to educate America's youth. Stephanie holds a certificate in pastoral leadership, a bachelor's degree in elementary education, and a master's of education degree in curriculum and instruction—reading.

In her free time, Stephanie enjoys writing, reading, surfing the web, painting on canvas, creating woodcrafts, and entrepreneurship. Her future aspiration is to write more books and travel the world. She is also the author of, Behold, I Give unto You Power, an inspirational book. Learn more about the author on most social media outlets.

Notes

Notes

Notes

Notes

Notes

Notes

Notes

Printed in the United States
by Baker & Taylor Publisher Services